Actionable SEO

Useful Tips & Tricks

by Shuaib Masoud

DesignLove.co.uk

Actionable SEO: Useful Tips + Tricks

Author: Shuaib Masoud

Written: 2013 Published: 2014

Menu

__Introduction__

Welcome to Actionable SEO: Useful Tips + Tricks

In this guide you will learn SEO Tips by going through some of the top SEO tips out there for big online traffic gains and in turn, boost sales from these visitors.

We will walk you through this guide in an easy to follow manner with real-world examples and tips that you can incorporate into your work right away for online success.

Note: In each tip you will see 'For you to try'. This is the part of the tip, which you can try in your own work and see results in real life. You will be glad you tried it!

Preface

SEO stands for Search Engine Optimisation. It is a methodology for driving traffic and although, you can find traffic in other ways, if your SEO is not developed completely you can lose out on the traffic that is sent to your site from search engines. So what should you be aiming for with SEO development? The answer is: Your website to be displayed on page 1 on major search engines such Google, Bing, Yahoo and others. From this, you will get lots of traffic, and in turn customers. The bottom line is, if you're not page 1 of search engine results page's (SERPs), your chances of gaining traffic will be reduced by a large margin.

Examples in this book

Throughout this book, we will use a small imaginary company that specialises in building services and repair and it will be called building services which is based in an imaginary city called Ronillet. This business serves both private property and commercial buildings. The website address for this will be www.buildingservices.co.uk. However, you have to remember that these 10 SEO tips in this book, are applicable to *any* company in *any* industry.

Tip #1: Search Engine friendly URLs

URLs are important. They are so important, as bad URLs can affect your search engine results and overall SEO success. This is because URLs need to be what is known as 'Search Engine Friendly', which is where URLs are easy to interpret and process for search engines. Also if a URL is search engine friendly chances are a human can read them easily too. The most important thing to remember is that now, modern search engine algorithms especially in Google's algorithm, want URLs to be readable by humans for the Google search engineer to consider it as a search engine friendly URL. However on Google's end further work will be done such as analysis before URL ranking is determined. Remember search engines will also want to know if the URL, Website, blog it is ranking also contains useful content for users. After all if the content is not liked by users the ranking of the website will be reduced. For us, correct and useful URLs should be the first step when developing your SEO strategy.

For You To Try:

The first thing for you to do, is to complete a technical check, making sure your site's main pages are coded in HTML/HTML5 instead of Flash. The reason Flash is a bad idea is because most search engines cannot read flash content, so important content such as META data, website titles, description and tags, will not be seen. So you can use all types of coding/scripting languages such as HTML, HTML5, PHP, ASP, Bootstrap, JavaScript etc. as long as you are able to add META and HTML information. Once that's done, you can begin working on URLs and check the URL coding. URLs are also known as Hyperlinks or just 'links'. URLs need to be 'search engine friendly' for search engines to be able to put them in categories to make the search engine's job easier when searching and displaying them to a user. This is known as search indexing. The final stage is when the search engine then displays the search results.

For example the following domain name and URL is fine: www.buildingservices.co.uk, and nothing could be changed here for it to be search engine friendly as it is the main URL. However, let's say you have a new web page file on the same website or server, and we called this new web page new3983u3.html. To access this webpage or file, we would now have to go to www.buildingservices.co.uk/new3983u3.html. From our example you can see it's a new web page because of the full stop html suffix (.html) afterwards. As we can see we do not know what the new web page is about with a name like that and to fix this, you should change the new web page to a name that is more useful such as 'how-to-order.html'. This new name will now tell search engines that the new URL is now www.buildingservices.co.uk/how-to-order.html and the Search Engine will understand that this is some sort of ordering instructions for the website. This is now a search engine friendy URL. Users, will also have a better idea of what the new URL is about before even visiting the webpage, thus increasing their chances of clicking on it.

Below you can see two examples of URL in the web browsers address bar, one is a friendly URL and one is an unfriendly URL. So this will give you a good idea of what you should be achieving when trying out this tip.

A bad or unfriendly URL example:

← → C 🗋 https://graph.facebook.com/me?sdk=ios&sdk_version=2&access_token=123902817987|8cb9e8408d2685cef853cd80.9

```
{
  "error": {
```

A good or friendly URL example:

← → C 🗋 www.2createawebsite.com/traffic/search-engine-traffic.html

 2 Create a Website
Don't Just Create a Website. Create a Web Business.

HOME   CREATE YOUR WEBSITE   MY BLOG   WEB DESIGN TIPS   120+ WEBSITE TOOLS $1.99 DOMAINS

Start Your Website   ▷

Create a WordPress Blog

WordPress (Blogging) Tips

Getting Listed & Ranked in Google, Yahoo and Bing

Home >> Get Traffic >> Getting Listed in Google, Bing and Yahoo

TIP #2: Keywords Research

Google AdWords
Keyword Planner

Plan your Search Network campaigns and
learn what your customers are looking for

To help you with the Adwords Research you can use a tool like Google Adwords Keywords Planner.

Keyword research is an integral part of SEO development. Without the correct wording, your business will not be linked to any keywords and without being linked to any keywords, the website is being prevented from showing up on results in the first place. So what is keyword research? Keyword Research is an area of SEO that involves a two-step process. In the first, you have to select specific keywords that are relevant to your business' products & services, or any words that mean something to your website's users. Two, once you have a list of your keywords, you now need to implement them into you website or blog, in content, text or multimedia, in such a way that search engines recognise your website as a website that contain information about your specific keywords. The main aim for successful keyword's, is to think of keywords that your potential leads and customers are likely to use and search for. For example, for our business Building Services, our example keywords can be:

1. Building services and repair

2. Building repairs

3. Property repairs and maintenance

4. Building repair and maintenance

As you can see the above keywords describe our business, but there probably will many companies offering similar services using the same keyword. So the keywords may be fine, but will be saturated and have a lot of competition. Unless your business is in an industry which is small or is rare, i.e. niche, you will want to avoid keywords that have too much competition. So what you will want to do at this stage is pick keywords that narrow the search results and if you want to take things to the next level, you have to be more specific. For example let's say Building Services, also fixes glass roofs (any type of glass including tempered glass), you can then include in your list keywords such as:

1. Tampered glass roof repairs

2. Tampered glass roof repair and maintenance

3. Building services & glass repair

4. Building glass repair

5. Glass roof repair

6. Roof building glass repair and maintenance

7. Glass roof repair and maintenance

The new set of keywords above narrow your search results by a margin, and hopefully a big margin. Now, why do you want the results to be narrowed? Well the simple answer is that if the results are narrowed, it means less search results and less pages on results and this in turn will mean less competition and increase your chance of ranking higher and possibly even on page 1 or 2. Remember when you're doing research, just because results are narrowed for certain keywords, it doesn't mean those keywords will work for your website. However, you can reverse the process and build a website or blog, based on keywords that have low competition, BUT you will need to be trustworthy and actually serve those keywords by the right products and services and/or content on your website or blog.

Now, for really interesting and successful keywords, we will step it up yet another gear. You can use keywords, which target a certain geographic location or particular demographics or advanced products or services or all. For example, if our building services business is based in Ronillet and we want to target office buildings only, we can use the following keywords separately or combined:

1. Office building services repair Ronillet

2. Office building repair maintenance Ronillet

3. Ronillet door builders and repair

4. Building repair Ronillet

The new and final keywords list, has been narrowed down by a lot and will specifically target offices and domestic homes in Ronillet that need building or door services, repair and maintenance.

It all depends what Ronillet has to offer, for instance another keyword can be window ledges repair Ronillet if Ronillet actually offer window ledge repairs. You just have figure out what will be useful for your website based on the services and products your offer and to whom it is targeted at, and from the above we can see we are targeting locals and local offices in Ronillet.

Another good way to beat the competition in search engines is if you offer advanced products or services, which means your business offers products and services that are innovative and or are a first in their industry. For example, let's say our company offers a new product they have developed, called roof cleaner, which is an automatic robot which cleans glass roofs without falling down with its advanced technology and the robot is called, GlassRoof Cleaner.

The keywords you can concentrate on can be:

1. Innovative glass roof cleaning product & services

2. Glass roof robotic cleaner

3. Robot glass roof cleaner

Now that's it for keyword research. As you can see it is a process that is always changing and always requires research and development and keyword maintenance, where you check if your keywords are still ranked high in search engines, if they bring you more traffic than your competition, how well they match your products & services, and checking the content on your website or blog user lands on is useful and for purpose.

Keyword research is a very important part of SEO, so work hard on it and results will follow shortly. This is a critical and principal part of organic SEO.

For you to do:

Useful steps for researching and developing your keywords strategies.

1. Build a list for your keywords - Make sure they relate to your products & services content, in this case we will build for the building & services company. For an example we can use all of the above and more just depending on what works for you i.e. what brings in traffic.

2. Look for a way to implement these keywords in your website or blog's content, texts, images, videos, images' titles and Meta description and the same for videos and audio. Remember for a further boost in traffic to also include in your website a good amount of images, videos, and audio content (around 3 per page) of your products or services, yourself, your team, and other similar products or services in your industry. For instance something that could be useful to your users for instance this could be a picture of an engineer repairing a building

3. Remember the best way to see results from keywords is to implement in a blog - This way you can add and change your content and keywords as often as you like without users expecting static information like on a website or about page

Keyword research can be broken down into to a three stage plan, 70-20-10; 70% of the work is the researching part and brainstorming, **think of it as if you starting a new business and you have to brainstorm ideas whether they will work or not**. 20% is the stage where you do the actual work (i.e. implementation into your website or blog), and the final 10% is where you maintain your keywords strategy over time.

TIP #3 META Data

In this section we will look at your META Data or Information, which is the technical data that provides metadata about the web page and tells search engines what your web pages on your website are about.

Meta tags are written in the <meta> tag, which is in HTML. Metadata is not displayed on the visual side of web pages, but instead in the code and is only viewed by computers and specialist software. The data itself includes details of the web page such as description, keywords, author of the document, last date of modification, and other information. The actual location of it in web pages is inside the web page's <head> tag.

Here is a good Metadata example looks like this:

```
<head>
<meta name="description" content="Building Services & Repairs">
<meta name="keywords" content="building repairs, office building repairs in
edinburgh, glass roof repair & maintenance">
<meta name="author" content="DesignLove">
<meta charset="UTF-8">
</head>
```

As you can see in the description section above, there is content that describes what our webpage is about and other small bits of technical information. The description section provides a brief description as to what the webpage is about, the keywords provides the key words included or should be included in the web page and also used for describing the genre of our web page/website. Finally the author is reserved for the name of the author of the web page.

A great Meta description, will include the field or industry the website is in i.e. for us it is Building services and repair, and the keywords should also match this. For instance 'building repair 'you can see in the description, is what describes what our webpage is about and other small bits of technical information.

For you to do:

In the Meta Tags in your HTML files, include in the description what your main services and products are, and in the keywords enter again your main products and services as well as your main keywords of the industry your serving. The web page's title should also be something appropriate such as 'I offer property building services and repair' etc. The web page's title should be ideally the same as the META Tag's title.

Below is an illustration showing the Metadata from DesignLove.co.uk.

```
<!DOCTYPE html>
<html lang="en">
  <head>
    <title>DesignLove Edinburgh - Web Design Packages - Buy Web Design Templates</title
    <meta name="viewport" content="width=device-width, initial-scale=1.0">
    <meta charset="utf-8">
    <link rel="stylesheet" href="CSS/bootstrap.css" media="screen">
    <link rel="stylesheet" href="CSS/assets/css/bootswatch.min.css">


<script src="galleria/galleria-1.3.2.min.js"></script>


    <!-- HTML5 shim and Respond.js IE8 support of HTML5 elements and media queries -->
    <!--[if lt IE 9]>
      <script src="../bower_components/html5shiv/dist/html5shiv.js"></script>
      <script src="../bower_components/respond/dest/respond.min.js"></script>
    <![endif]-->
    <script type="text/javascript">
```

TIP #4: YouTube and YouTube Videos

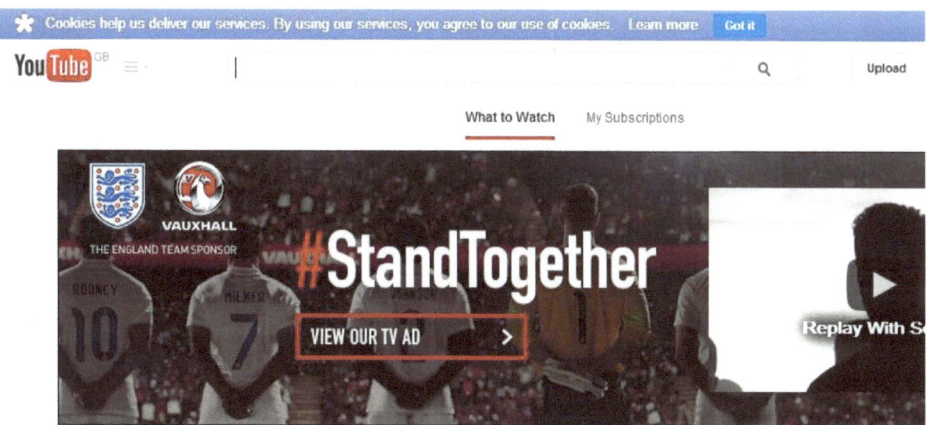

Recommended

YouTube.com is one of the top site's online today.

YouTube as many of you might know is the biggest video sharing website. Infact YouTube is also a huge search engine in own its rights (source: wwww,2012) so big, it is the second biggest search engine, ever. Taken over by Google in 2008, and its easy to see why it was,
with video being a such a big media format in general. When you take videos online and coupled with a solid & robust social sharing platform that keeps growing by the day, you give YouTube traffic that is unheard of in the record books. Look at the stats below and your mind will be blown at how loud they speak:

4 Billion Daily Video Views Stats, http://www.reuters.com/article/2012/01/23/us-google-youtube-idUSTRE80M0TS20120123, 2012

So what's so special about YouTube so much that we need to consider it in our Top Ten SEO Tips? Why not use another video sharing platform? (Yes in reality we can but the stats speak for themselves alone and YouTube can bring enormous amount of traffic to your website. There are two ways which have worked great for many people including myself. The reason I say these two are top ways of driving traffic because they have driven the most amount traffic to my real website blog.designlove.co.uk. The two methods are: video and the video embed option in upload and the second method is YouTube keyword and video Meta data. I will cover what these are. The video method actually just means any video uploaded to YouTube and setting it up in a way that it is embeddable on external sites. What this means is that once your video is successful uploaded it can be embedded by anyone on any other site thus providing a great indirect 'link' back to your site. The second method is optimising your video in YouTube so well that it comes on the top of the video results on the video search and other search engines externally. This leads people back to your channel and website if done correctly and targeted right.

Be warned this tip is longer than normal! Because video is longest media format so a more in-depth explanation was needed.

For you to do:

Okay, let's get on it with it. For us to get on YouTube you will first need a video. Yes you may have heard of 'viral' videos of for instance a very low flying jet or a cat that's gone crazy. But these videos are just that, merely fun. They were made for fun and that's not our goal here. Even though we might get very little views compared to these types of videos we are not worried and our aim is business, leads and conversion, so we need business videos. So you will need to create a video. It should only be to do with something in your business industry. Here is an example video template: blog.designlove.co.uk/top-ten-seo-tips-video-template. Let's say our example could be laying bricks for beginners: brick laying tips and you can have a good 'SEO' friendly title such as 'Brick Laying Tips: Step by Step for Beginners'. The video content of this could be: You or another professional in your firm safely demonstrating how to brick lay. Including techniques for beginners, being the emphasis of the whole video content. So you should say things like 'Beginners start with this technique',' If you are a beginner this technique will be difficult but can be mastered' etc. If you sell bricks you can add value and increase sales if you show the bricks you sell near the end of the video. The actual visual parts of the video should have a structure. Just like a well written book, our video will start with for example an intro animation, then an introduction from a spokesperson or the builder himself, then the main job and tips, then an outro where its important to thank the viewers and tell them how they can get more tips or contact your business (on screen details are great), and maybe some products or services your firm offers at the end of the video.

Once your video is all recorded and edited you upload it to YouTube. Uploading is easy and you can find a tutorial on our site here: blog.designlove.co.uk/how-to-upload-videos-YouTube-for-beginners. Be patient on this step as it can take quite a while to upload and for YouTube, to do final checks. You should be on the setup and upload page on YouTube. Now the most important step here is checking the option which is called: Allow video to be embedded on to other external sites. It is crucial that you check this option or you won't receive any traffic to your website from your video. With this option checked your video can be embedded on lots websites and especially high-traffic video sharing websites, meaning it is a link back to your YouTube channel and direct link to your site if the URL is embedded in the description or title (more on this coming up shortly). By allowing others to embed it on their websites and applications, you're making an opportunity for hundreds more views to be gained . Now let's move on to step two (second method).

Once the video is finished uploading you will still be on the upload/details page of your video and YouTube will not re-direct you to any other page. This is great because it's the page we need. If you're not on this page please go to it by clicking on your video, then click on' Edit Video'. You should now be on the edit details page. Now what we want to do here is key in the details (or META data if you're looking for the technical term). The three things we need to concentrate on are: Title, Description, and the Keywords.

The title has to be descriptive and SEO friendly, too. Our example of 'Brick Laying Tips: Step by Step for Beginners' is perfect because it does exactly what it says on the title. It will pop in results for searches containing keywords such as 'brick laying' even more so for 'brick laying tips' and it should definitely be high on with keywords 'brick laying tips step by steps' or possibly number one or top five results for 'brick laying tips step by step for beginners'. Why? Let me explain. When someone searches with keywords that match our title and our title is optimised for search i.e. SEO, it means that our video or page has a higher chance than anyone else's video of showing up higher.

The **Description** is next. This is probably the next most important part, especially from a user's perspective since most users first usually see and read the title then the description. This section should describe the video in as much detail as possible but using as little words as possible. A good example could be: "By www.buildingservices.co.uk/bricklaying. Brick Laying Tips: Step by Step for Beginners is an easy to follow video packed with techniques for a beginner in brick laying". The key criteria to consider are including the keywords and keeping it concise. The description should be no longer than 3-4 lines.

Lastly is the **Tags/Keywords**, which should be easy. All the keywords included are keywords from the title and description. So if you include something here in keywords; but it's not in the description or title, then make sure to add it in. What will you include in the keywords? Pick out the main or keywords in the title and description (these are SEO friendly keywords not normal keywords!): brick, brick laying, brick laying tips, brick laying beginners, brick laying step by step. As you can see our keywords will also help in the search results whether in Google or YouTube itself because it includes the actual keywords from our title, description, and they describe the video content very well.

Here is what the title, description and keywords should like in the end:

Title: **Brick Laying Tips: Step by Step for Beginners**
Description: **By www.buildingservices.co.uk/bricklaying. Brick Laying Tips: Step by Step for Beginners is an easy to follow video packed with techniques for a beginner in brick laying.**
Tags: **brick, brick laying, brick laying tips, brick laying beginners, brick laying step by step**

Further work: You should now expect more users going to your website! So watch your views go up and up. One thing I will say is be consistent and don't try these techniques on another video website until after a year or so or until you have lots and lots of new customers coming from your YouTube channel.

TIP: Include a link like I did in our example as one of the first things on the first line of our description. This will provide a clean sharp link that hits the user first thing when they read the description so they can quickly go to your site should they want to and also forms a great 'engagement product' as you're allowing the user to see what goes on outside your YouTube videos and channel and be involved in your website.

For those who want to build a brand whether just an online brand or offline, on the title, description and tags you should include a business name. So for example ours could look like:

Title: **Brick Laying Tips: Step by Step for Beginners - By Building Services**
Description: **www.buildingservices.co.uk/bricklaying. Building Services brings you Brick Laying Tips: Step by Step for Beginners is an easy to follow video packed with techniques for the beginner**

in brick laying. We only show you the basics and this video is great for new starts. Watch now to experience beginner tips in brick laying.

Tags: brick, brick laying, brick laying tips, brick laying beginners, brick laying step by step

Tip #5: Landing Page

You have probably heard of landing pages but you don't know what they are or how to use them. A 'landing page' is a page that can easily convert a visit to into a sale. So basically this can be the first page of your site or the middle or the last, it doesn't really matter. What is a landing page? A landing page is any standard web page on your website that requires the visitor to part with something, either payment for a product or service or an email address for RSS subscription. After you have this you will need a form whether it's for signing up to product information or a buy now button or subscription button you pay for monthly website login. Either way, once a customer fills in this form and subscribes to your product or service or buys it straight away, your landing page has proved to be successful. But there's more to it.

For you to do:

For capturing new sales prospects via email create a new page called e.g. 'sign-up.html' You will need web development experience if you have to upload this to your web server (where all your site data is stored). If you want your visitors to buy a product or charge them for subscribing to your website, you can call this page for 'new-product.html' or something more specific 'building-tools.html' or 'monthly-subscribe-here.html'. Once you have a page in place and set up its time to focus on the actual content. For the email subscriptions all you need on this page at the minimum is a short introduction explaining why you need to capture the email address. For example:

''Enter your email address below for FREE WEEKLY UPDATES right to your inbox! Sign up now to make sure you don't miss out.''

And a simple form where the visitor enters their email address. That's it! For the product for sale or charged subscription you need a simple introduction again and a simple shopping basket, PayPal pay now button or subscription button. Yes that's it for this type of page too. Now that your page is designed and developed, to make this into what's known as a real landing page, all you do is the following steps. On any external website, whether it's a comment or replying to an email or a directory entry, all you do is direct potential customers directly to your landing page. For example:

For the best FREE WEEKLY OFFERS go to: www.buildingservices.co.uk/sign-up.html.

Online example:

Go to www.buildingservices.co.uk/ building-tools.html now to get our latest product online!

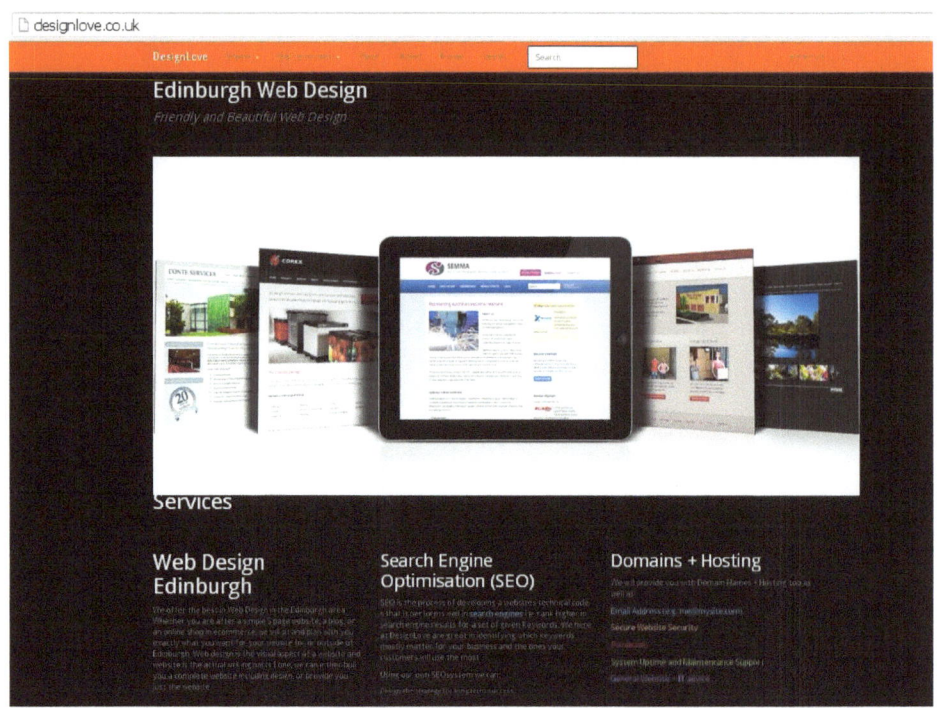

A home page can be a good landing page too if done correctly. Above is Designlove.co.uk which has a form for quotes on the same page. You can get to this form if you click on Quote. Below is a screenshot of how the Quote section looks like:

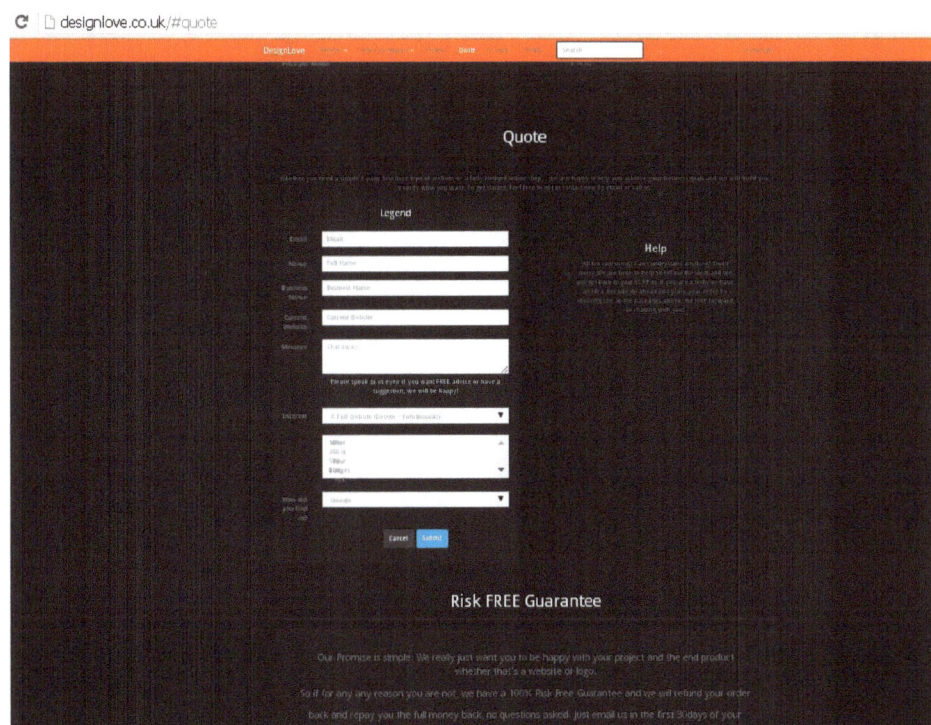

Quote

Risk FREE Guarantee

Our Promise is simple. We really just want you to be happy with your project and the end product whether that's a website or logo.

So if for any any reason you are not, we have a 100% Risk Free Guarantee and we will refund your order back and repay you the full money back, no questions asked. Just email us in the first 30 days of your order even if you are the slightest worried and want your money back.

Review Packages

Tip #6: Useful Tools

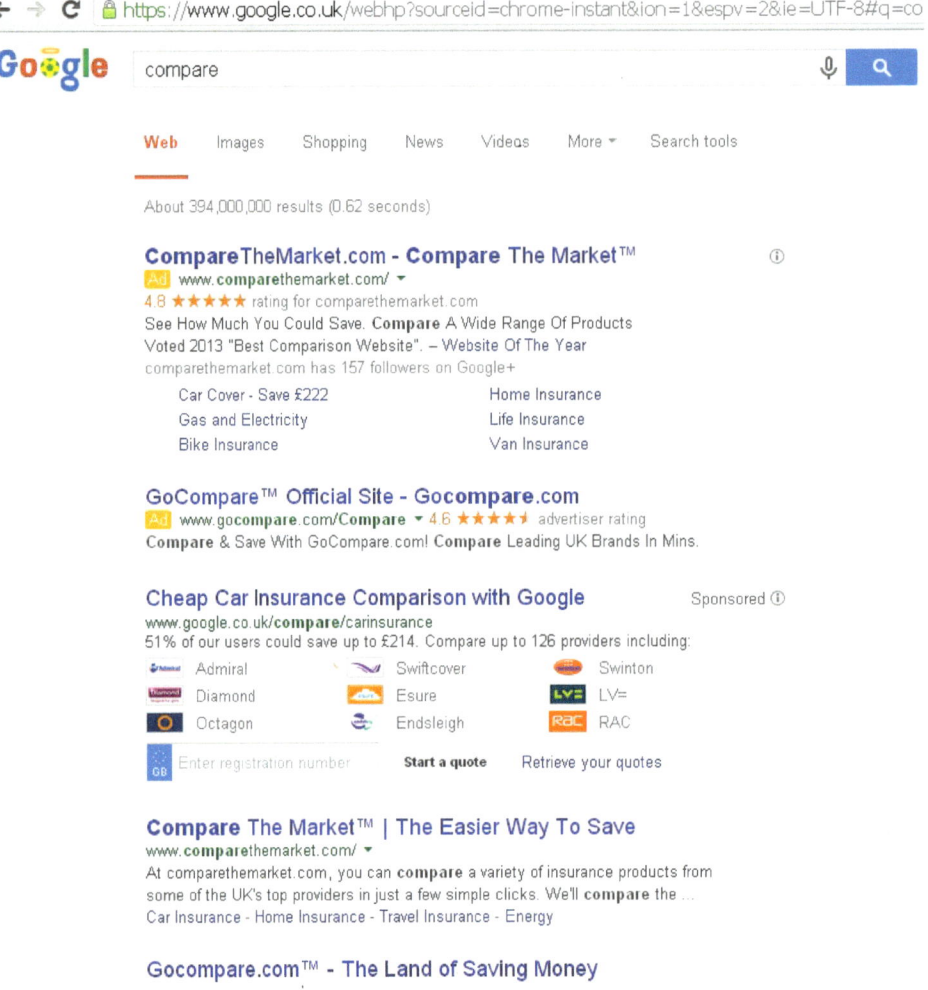

The internet is flooded with online tools these days; some of the top are comparison tools. Google itself acts a good comparison tool when shopping with Google Shopping Google.com/shopping.

This tip is about creating or acquiring a tool that is useful in your industry, this tool has to be related to your products and services or somewhat close. For example there is no point offering free milk if you sell car parts, but it will be suitable to offer free milk if you're in the dairy business or are a retailer that sells milk. The type of free tool can also be a variety of things of which its aim should be a tool that helps the website's visitors a lot or even a little. For example some finance and accounting firms offer financial calculators.

What for?

Because for one they either found your website or they like your website and are a repeat visitor because of this tool. They could have found your website through the way we want them too i.e. search terms or came straight after given word of mouth by a friend or someone else. Either way, if someone visits your website because of a free tool they find useful, this is a great thing regardless of where you rank for the page of the free tool, as this will drive traffic anyway and the increase can be incredible sometimes.

Useful tools are meant to help users and if a user visits your blog/website and found the tool useful then this is like an extra 'point' for you.

The best useful free tool in my eyes is Google's Search Engine (and I think it is for many too!). Another example of a great free tool price comparison website or a mortgage calculator, these are all useful free tools.

And don't be surprised when you see their websites have lots of traffic!

For you to try

What you will have to do as mentioned above is either develop your own tool from scratch or acquire one by buying one that has full rights. Chances are if its an online tool, it will be classified as software, meaning you will need a license for it. For our example we are going to create a fuel usage calculator and integrate this to our website so users can use it and hopefully find it useful.

We can create one by doing the following:

1. Use a programming or scripting language such as **VB.NET**,PHP, or JavaScript to create the calculator

2. Create a new page for it on our website

3. Integrate this onto our website

4. Have an option for users to download it so they can use it without being on the Internet

5. You don't even have to create a calculator. For instance we can create a search tool or a comparison tool, or a location/branch tool etc., the list goes on

Now the above might be complicated but

Extra help:
Download our free calculator or ask us to make you a custom one! You can download ours from our blog at www.blog.designlove.co.uk.

And remember about the old saying 'Content is King'. Your content has to be useful to your visitors. Full stop. If it's not then your website will not be worth visiting or previous visitors will not return.

Tip #7: Retention of Traffic

Retention of traffic is about striking a balance between useful resources and products and services, so that your customers always want to come back time after time. In this section we will talk about what's important to keep visitors (and hopefully customers) coming back to your website without you doing any much direct communication requests such as individual email/letters where you specifically ask each person to visit your site. Because let's face it, it's difficult, if not impossible to ask every visitor to your site individually. The main issue with this is that you have to spend hours either manually sorting out traffic or using software, to find out first which visit out of the traffic was a real human and which was just a robot, such as a search engine spider or other web service. Then stage two of this is finding process is discovering who, out of the visits, visited your website intentionally and are interested, rather than 'accidental' traffic i.e. didn't know they were coming to your website. Lastly you would need to email/contact each person individually and try to convince them to visit your site, and we can safely say some people just don't reply or ever visit or ever open your email/pick up your call etc.

So what's the solution?

To get around this, the best thing to do is just to do what you already are doing, add great quality content to your website regularly and have a site that has products and services that customers need or want, but the key to keeping this going is after around 6 months or so of your website running and trying to retain traffic is to add 'little extras' such as free gifts and freebies which as long they are specific to your industry can be anything you want e.g. from free instructional manuals, to free web templates, free tires, free brake checks etc., free etc.

For you to do:

After running your website for around 6 months and have kept at adding good quality content and articles, you could add freebies, downloads buttons, offer free code etc, basically it should be based on whatever your site offers. For example if you sell meat, offer discount vouchers etc. The free resources can be on the home page to catch more attention, or in other new separate pages and if need be make a very slight change the design of your website, so you can accommodate the freebies and other resources.

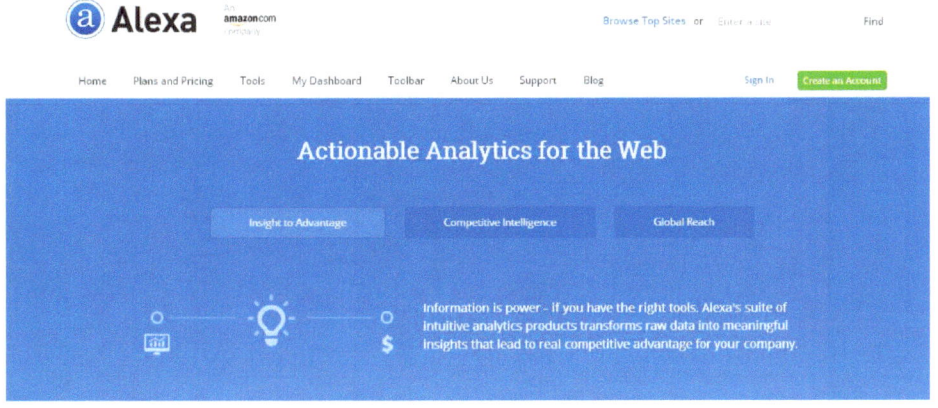

You should also keep checking is your hard work paying off by monitoring your previous, current, and new traffic numbers and sources. Above is Alexa.com, by Amazon, is a great tool to find out your current traffic, new traffic, back-links, as well useful for checking whether your traffic is increasing or decreasing. If your traffic is increasing, chances are your website is doing well at retaining the current traffic and on top of this includes new traffic.

Tip #8: Follow the leader

Global	1	Google.com
		Enables users to search the world's information, including webpages, images, and videos. Offers... More
By Country	2	Facebook.com
By Category		A social utility that connects people, to keep up with friends, upload photos, share links and ... More
	3	Youtube.com
		YouTube is a way to get your videos to the people who matter to you. Upload, tag and share your... More
	4	Yahoo.com
		A major internet portal and service provider offering search results, customizable content, cha... More
	5	Baidu.com
		The leading Chinese language search engine, provides "simple and reliable" search exp... More
	6	Wikipedia.org
		A free encyclopedia built collaboratively using wiki software. (Creative Commons Attribution-Sh... More
	7	Qq.com
		China's largest and most used Internet service portal owned by Tencent, Inc founded in Nov... More
	8	Taobao.com
		Launched in May 2003, Taobao Marketplace (www.taobao.com) is the online shopping destination of... More
	9	Twitter.com
		Social networking and microblogging service utilising instant messaging, SMS or a web interface.
	10	Live.com
		Search engine from Microsoft.

Above are the top websites online as of June 2014, Alexa.org.

This is probably one of the most useful tips I can give. Following the leader or leaders in your industry and niche, is invaluable. These are guys who have been there and tried it, who know what works and what doesn't, failed before (at least once), and now are at the top of their game. With that said, you need to pay very close attention of what they do and how they do it.

So let's take a look at the pros and cons of following the leader/s in your industry. The first advice we would give is to find out if your definition of the 'leader' really means the 'leader' by pointing to someone who is successful in your industry in terms of a two main principles:

Success in business – Lots of sales, customers, and profit

Success in research & information – Quality research turns into successful prototypes, products, services, and information is 'power'.

The first point above is basically rule number one, even though previously we have said it generally takes time for success for any business of any shape or format or industry, it does not mean you cannot follow in the footsteps of someone who already is or almost is. There is big gap for beginners in web businesses to established websites which are literally about to be successful or already are, this is why we do not need to worry to the fact that it could take long to be successful online but rather worry about whether you are trying to do the same as the leaders in your industry. Which is far more important, as you what you are trying to do has probably already been done before.

Following someone else will enable you to propel your road to success much faster than not following. The great things you can pick up by following the leader are many, but here are a few to think about:

1.   Learn what products & services sell

2.   Learn how their products & services are created, sourced, managed, introduced, marketed, and offered

3.   Learn what research they are doing that keeps them leading

4.   Learn what mistakes they have made, so you can avoid them

From the above you can see that by following someone you will learn how to be successful and because you will be following the leader in your industry, the above will most likely if done correctly and in the same or similar way as the company you chose and who you see as the leader. You will also know what will not work so well as if it is something that can work well, and then the leading business will be offering it.

For you to do:

Sleep on your competition's website at the end of each day, for at-least 1 year. What we mean by that is that you have to be consistently watching your competition's website a few times a month, if not daily. This will give you a feeling of what your site should look like, to steal traffic from links or contacts

Make a list of the top 10 web businesses/offline in your industry. They must have a website though for them to be useful for you. Then tone this down to 5, by filtering out the less successful ones. Then further cut this down to the top 3, and this is where you need to bookmark these 3 and then study them. The first thing to do is to research and collect information in the following areas below:
1.   Market including chosen niche if it applies
2.   Products & Services offered – including pricing, target market
3.   Website name & character length of name
4.   Website http address
5.   Website & colour theme
6.   Website technology used
7.   Website number of pages, names

TIP #9: Local Keyword Optimisation

Local and hyper-local keyword optimisation is the process of optimising keywords on search engines that are local places in your city or surrounding areas, Boroughs, villages and towns.
Hyper local is locations that are is even closer places like streets, shops or shopping centres or markets or areas of attractions.

So how is local and hyper-local keyword optimisation done? Let's take local keyword optimisation first.

Local Marketing is important for your website's success offline and online.

For you to do:

Get a paper and pen, and draw a 2 column table with 2 rows, making the 2nd row much bigger than the 1st. This can be done in Excel or a word table too on a computer. Now in the first row in the left hand side, title it 'Products + Services' and in right hand side call it 'Place'.

Now all you need to do is list all your products and services that you offer on your website in the second row under products & services. Once you have done that list down the busiest boroughs next to your products. So if you have car tires for instance you can have it like this: car tires: Kensington, or house bricks: Wembley etc. You have got to be smart here and may need to match these products services against other places in your city depending on the areas with higher populations and /or where people live who buys the product or service the most.

Once you competed your list which matches the products and services for the boroughs or place in your city, the thing you need to do is add them to together to make your keyword into one. So for instance building services for Ronnillet the geographic area equals to Ronnillet building services and this will be your local keyword, car tires Kensington. Do the same for all your keywords and then the list will be complete.

Next, you take your list of keywords and create a new page or add it to existing pages relating to the product or service. The important thing to do here is to make sure it'll fit together. So firstly ensure your page is only including the local keyword so for example the website buildingsrrvices.co.uk will have a page called house bricks and the URL will be house-bricks-kensington.html and on the website when visiting the page it will look like buildingservices.o.uk/house-bricks-kensington.html.

Remember to include other places too like surrounding towns or villages but I would say keep it within a 15 mile radius, otherwise it won't be local any more. Another local marketing area is hyper-local keyword optimisation. This is very similar to the local keyword optimization however the only difference being that you will now look at local places **in depth** like a local shop or street. Once implemented, your website should start to see an increase in traffic and sales too.

Remember I've only touched on this area, so do more research and read into businesses that target local markets.

Tip 10: The Top Tip of them All

I would say it all boils down to three crucial factors for online success. These are the three ingredients that determine whether or not a website will be successful. This is my honest opinion, and it's as simple as that. The first; is that you need to put in time, as it can take years of hard work and 95% of the time, online success has no shortcuts and no overnight success stories. Two, you also need the right tangibles, even though we are talking about websites and the digital world, your website need's to have the right content and/or be selling the right products and services, whether for money or information (contact details of customers through forms etc.). Lastly, the third factor is, you guessed it, traffic. Simply put, without traffic, you have no visitors, and with no visitors you have no leads, and lastly with no leads you have no sales.

For you to do:

1. Don't be afraid to fail. You can keep trying but on a new or similar idea for a business website

2. Be consistent – Better to do little content and done often over a long time, than a lot of content created once per year

3. Drive more traffic – If you follow Tips 1,2,3,4,5,6,7, 8 and 9, you website will bound to receive plenty of traffic for years to come and success will follow too

Conclusion

First of all apologies it has taken so long to finish the book project, now I know what it really means when top writers say 'writing takes longer than you think' as I thought I initially would have finished this project within 6 months, then there was more work done so I thought maybe in another 3-4 months, then maybe 6months again. But as you can see all in all this book was written in months!

That I aside, I hope you truly enjoy it and view it as a great addition from the first book I wrote, I think many people will find great use for it for their websites. Even though the theme is similar to the first four page release I did but this is a lot more in-depth. Although overnight results are impossible and not promised, but as with most things that are to be successful in life, I have learned that you need persistence; hard work, business people networking, integrity and research, research, research and it will all soon pay off.

What next?
I could possibly improve on this release post feedback from you.

Join us:

www.facebook.com/designlove.co.uk
Twitter on @CheapDesigns
Youtube.com/mediaking11
Blog a blog.designlove.co.uk

References & Thanks:

W3Schools.com

Google.com

Wordpress.com

jQuery.com

YouTube.com

Flickr.com

Facebook.com

Twitter.com

Wikepedia.org

JavaScript

And Many Many Thanks to:

Napier.ac.uk (My former university)

Lisa Irby from www.2createawebsite.com for great tips

Bethie for her awesome editing work! – Contact details upon request

M A Uddin – Cover Design & Illustrator – Contact details upon request

Nasra Masoud – Grammar Edits – She is still a school student!

www.ingramcontent.com/pod-product-compliance
Lightning Source LLC
Chambersburg PA
CBHW050414180526
45159CB00005B/2271